discard

Ken Griffey, Jr.

BURTON ELEMENTARY
LIBRARY

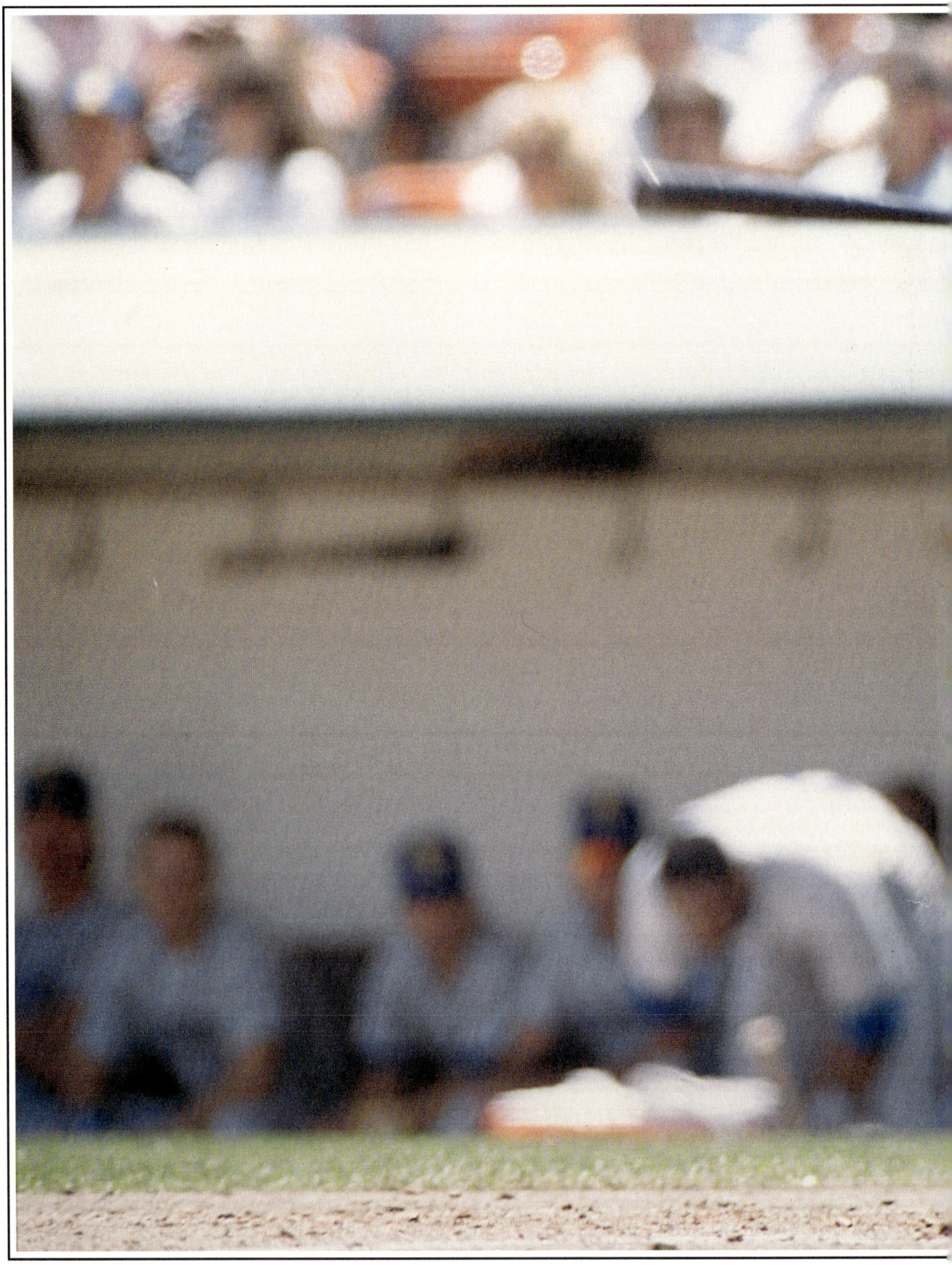

BURTON ELEMENTARY
LIBRARY

PHOTO CREDITS
Andrew Bernstein: (10)
Michael Zagaris: (5)

Text copyright © 1991 by The Child's World, Inc.
All rights reserved. No part of this book may be
reproduced or utilized in any form or by any means
without written permission from the Publisher.
Printed in the United States of America.

Distributed to Schools and Libraries
in the United States by
ENCYCLOPAEDIA BRITANNICA EDUCATIONAL CORP.
310 S. Michigan Avenue
Chicago, Illinois 60604

Library of Congress Cataloging-in-Publication Data
Rothaus, James.
  Ken Griffey, father and son / Jim Rothaus.
      p. cm.
  Summary: Presents sports profiles of Seattle Mariner baseball
    player, Ken Griffey, Jr., and his illustrious father,
  Ken Griffey, Sr., who played for several major league teams
         and now plays alongside his son.
            ISBN 0-89565-783-X
  1. Griffey, Ken–Juvenile literature. 2. Griffey, Ken, 1950-
    –Juvenile literature. 3. Baseball players–United States–
    Biography–Juvenile literature. [1. Griffey, Ken.
    2. Griffey, Ken, 1950-   . 3. Baseball players.] I. Title.
         GV865.A1R68 1991   91-24878
         796.357'092'2–dc20   CIP
             [B]   AC

★ Ken Griffey, Jr. ★

by James R. Rothaus

The face is new but the name is not.

Another All-Star Griffey

When the American League team took the field for the 1990 All-Star Game, there was a new face in center field. It belonged to twenty-year-old Ken Griffey Jr. of the Seattle Mariners. The face was new, but the name wasn't. Ten years before, Ken Griffey Sr. was the most valuable player of the All-Star Game. Griffey Sr. played for the Cincinnati Reds back then. He was later traded to the Atlanta Braves and then to the New York Yankees.

Father and Son on Same Team

In 1988 Ken Griffey Sr. was back with the Reds. Griffey Sr. stayed with Cincinnati until August of 1990, when the Reds let him go. But Ken Griffey Sr. wasn't without a team for long. He soon signed with the Seattle Mariners, who put him in left field. Next to Griffey Sr. in center field was his son, Ken Griffey Jr. It was the first time in major league baseball history that a father and son had played on the same team at the same time.

Seattle Mariners made a good deal.

Hottest young star in the Majors.

Who's Better, Father or Son?

Ken Griffey Sr. has had a great career. He has a lifetime batting average of .297. He also has a career total of more than 2,000 hits. As good as Ken Griffey Sr. has been, his son may be better. Junior, as the younger Griffey is known, may be the hottest young star in the majors. He became a starter with the Mariners in 1989 when he was only nineteen years old. In 1990 Ken Griffey Jr. batted .300. He hit twenty-two home runs and drove in eighty runs. He also made the All-Star Team.

Junior Is Bigger and Stronger

But Junior's biggest thrill in 1990 was getting to play with his father. It was a big thrill for Ken Griffey Sr., too. In fact Senior called it the best thing that's happened to him in his eighteen-year major league career. Senior had played on two World Series winning teams in Cincinnati. He had made the All-Star Game three times. Senior almost won a National League batting title in 1976. But his biggest thrill is watching his son. Junior is bigger and stronger than his father.

Junior can hit with power.

13

A defensive standout.

Junior and the Big Red Machine

Ken Griffey Jr. started playing in the majors when he was nineteen. But he had been around the big leagues and big league players since he was a little boy. Junior was three years old when his father began playing for Cincinnati in 1973. Cincinnati was known then as the Big Red Machine. The Red Machine won World Series titles in 1975 and 1976. Junior grew up around Cincinnati stars Johnny Bench, Pete Rose, Joe Morgan, and Tony Perez. "Junior has always thought of himself as a big-leaguer because that's all he remembers," Senior said.

Long Road to the Major Leagues

Ken Griffey Sr. had to work hard to make the majors. After he was drafted in 1969, it took him four years to make the big leagues. There were times that Senior wondered if he could make it to the majors. "Junior doesn't know what I went through to build my career," Senior said. But Ken Griffey Sr. did make it. He also wanted to make sure Junior would grow up to be a good person, and maybe even a major leaguer. Senior and his wife, Alberta, were strict parents. They didn't allow Junior to act up.

Junior grew up around the game.

Ken Jr. is proud of his Dad.

Mom Keeps Junior in Line

If Junior didn't do his homework, his mother wouldn't let him play baseball. One time Junior got so mad during a game that he threw his glove in anger. Mrs. Griffey walked over to the coach and told him to take Junior out of the game. Alberta Griffey then dragged her son home, where she told him never to do anything like that again. Junior grew up and became a great talent. When he graduated from high school, Junior was one of the best young players in the country.

First Pick in 1987 Draft

The Seattle Mariners knew how good Junior was. The Mariners had the first pick in the 1987 draft. Everyone was telling them to take Junior. The Mariners didn't need to be told. They wanted Griffey more than any other player. Junior was the first pick in the draft. Less than two years later, he was starting in center field for the Mariners. He was a kid among men. But this kid was having a ball. Baseball was just a game to Junior.

A great high school talent.

A kid among men.

Junior Just Wants to Have Fun

"We're always talking about going out there and having fun," said Gene Clines, hitting coach for the Mariners. "But few players do that. Junior has fun." Mariner manager Jim Lefebvre was glad his star was so happy-go-lucky. "Junior is a young, exciting player who truly enjoys playing the game. I hope that never changes. Too many players are too serious. It's nice to see somebody enjoy the game as much as he does."

Seattle's First Baseball Star

Junior became the Mariners' first true star. The team had been a member of the American League since 1977, but the Mariners were not that good. In their first fourteen years, the M's never had a winning season. But team officials believed that Junior and a bunch of good young pitchers would make the M's a pennant contender. In 1990 Junior had a good year, but the team won only seventy-seven games. Seattle finished fifth in the seven-team American League Western Division.

★ **A happy-go-lucky kind of guy.** ★

Young pitchers plus Junior = contender.

Just Do What He Does Best

When the 1991 season began, there were high hopes for the Mariners. One of the reasons was Ken Griffey Jr. He was a veteran at age twenty-one. He was also expected by some to be a leader. "I think the biggest mistake a team can make is asking someone to be a leader when it's not a natural thing for them to do," said Woody Woodward, Mariner vice president. "At this point of his career, all I want Junior to do is go out and play as many baseball games as he can and do what he does best."

Junior Is a Natural

Woodward knew that Griffey Jr. was still a big kid. Woodward also knew that it wasn't wise to force Junior to be a leader. "If leadership comes naturally to him, that's great," Woodward said. "But I don't see him becoming a take-charge guy in the clubhouse." That just isn't Junior's style. "I don't see myself ever telling other guys what to do," Junior said. Junior will just <u>show</u> other guys what to do. "I don't think anybody's ever been that good at that age," Gene Clines said. "He is a natural."

A veteran at twenty-one.

Ken Jr. leads All-Star balloting.

The Ken Griffey Jr. Candy Bar

He is also the only twenty-year-old baseball player in history to have a candy bar named after him. The Ken Griffey Jr. candy bar was sold during the 1990 season. Almost one million people bought the chocolate bar named for the first big star in Seattle Mariner history. But Junior has other goals besides having his own candy bar. He would like to make the Mariners the kind of team in the 1990s that the Cincinnati Reds were in the 1970s, back when his father was one of the Reds' stars.